NEW ZEALAND

A PANORAMIC EXPERIENCE

GARETH EYRES

THE
BACKROADS
PRESS

All Images: © Copyright Gareth Eyres
Exposure, P.O. Box 66-069, Beachhaven,
North Shore City, Auckland, New Zealand.
Web: www.exposure.co.nz
Ph: 0064 9 4837734
The Backroads Press
PO Box 66-069, Beachhaven,
North Shore City, Auckland, New Zealand.

Cover, Design and Production: Jaimée Clapham

Marketing: Chanel Publishers Ltd.,
P.O. Box 403, Whangaparaoa

Printed in China by Midas Printing (Asia) Ltd.
Distributed by Beckett Books.
Ph: 09 442 4438

ISBN 0-473-09858-X

Front cover: Last light at Cape Reinga.
Back cover: Aoraki Mt. Cook and Lake Pukaki viewed from Peter's lookout, on the Mt. Cook road.
End pages: Moody morning at Kaikoura.
Title page: Aotearoa Summer: A pohutakawa in full bloom near Matarangi, Coromandel Peninsula.

CONTENTS

THE COASTLINE

LONE RIDER: A surfer catches a perfect wave at Raglan.

Previous pages: TORRENT BAY: Tide mouldings scallop the shore in Abel Tasman National Park.

TALL STACK: Evening light paints the Pancake Rocks at Punakaiki.

Previous pages:
HOLIDAY DESTINATION: Pauanui on the Coromandel coast is
a popular escape for Aucklanders.

Opposite:
WHITE CLIFFS OF PORTLAND: Portland Island east of Mahia.

Above:
ZANE GREY'S PLAYGROUND: Urupukapuka Island in the Bay of Islands
was once the base of Zane Grey, famous American sport fisherman.

Right:
HOLE IN THE ROCK: Piercy Island off Cape Brett.

WHERE MOUNTAINS MEET THE SEA: Dawn overlooking the Seaward Kaikouras, with snow-covered Mt Manakau, 2609m high.

SAFE HAVEN: Castlepoint Lighthouse marks one of the few sheltered anchorages on the rugged Wairarapa Coast.

WHERE WE LIVE

SEASIDE SUBURB: Devonport on Auckland's North Shore.

Previous pages: DUSK OVER AUCKLAND: The Auckland Harbour Bridge from Northcote Point.

CITY SUNRISE: An aerial cityscape on a chilly September morning as the sun rises over Auckland.

CHAMPAGNE POOL: Rotorua is the thermal capital of New Zealand and home to 50,000 New Zealanders. Wai-O-Tapu Thermal Wonderland is one of the famous hotspots for tourists.

Following pages: BALLOONS OVER WAIKATO: Every autumn balloonists from around the world gather in Hamilton to display their talents and fly across the gentle Waikato farmland.

HARBOUR LIGHTS: Wellington is New Zealand's capital city, nestled around a perfect harbour.

HOUSES ON THE HILL: Villas nestle under Mt Victoria, Wellington.

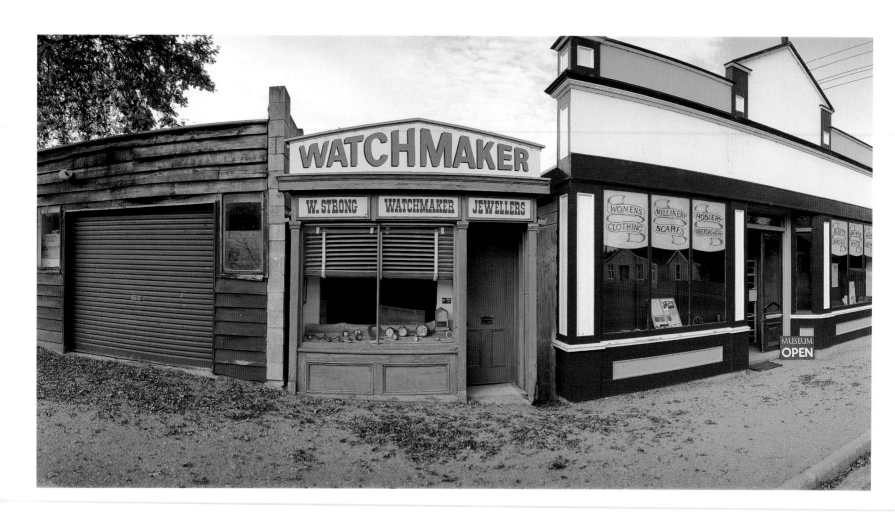

STREETS OF A TIME GONE BY: Naseby in Central Otago was once a bustling gold-mining town.

WINE COUNTRY: Hawkes Bay is one of New Zealand's premier winemaking areas.

DOWN ON THE FARM: Late muster on the Mesopotamia Station, Canterbury.

SCHOOL DAYS: Rugby training afternoon at Christchurch Boys' High.

FOREST AND RIVERS

Previous pages: RIVER OF GOLD: Tannins tint the rainforest on the West Coast of the South Island.

ARROWTOWN ABLAZE: Autumn sets the hillside above Arrowtown alight with warm, earthy colours.

THIS COULD BE MIDDLE EARTH: The Oparara region on the West Coast of the South Island is a mystical land of primeval forest and limestone stuctures.

VIEW FROM ABOVE: Ponga ferns at Lake Tarawera.

MAGNIFICENT MOUNT HOBSON: Walkers pause in the sub-tropical forest on Mt. Hobson, Great Barrier Island's highest point.

MAJESTIC KING COUNTRY FALLS: Marokopa Falls in full flow after winter rains.

Following pages: FROM THE LAKE TO THE OCEAN: Huka Falls is the first set of falls on the Waikato River as it heads north from Lake Taupo to the sea at Port Waikato.

A LAND OF ACTIVITIES

DOWNTOWN CLIMBER: The volcanic cliffs near Auckland Boys Grammar School offer a natural urban experience.

Previous pages: CRUISING THE ABEL TASMAN: The Abel Tasman National Park is a great sea kayaking destination as well as a walking paradise.

Far right top: WEST COAST WONDERLAND: New Zealand is custom-made for a motorhome holiday ... quiet roads, good camping areas with no shortage of things to do and people to meet.

ALL ABOARD AND UPRIGHT: Another raft successfully runs the waterfall on the Kaituna River near Rotorua.

THE ISLANDS OF THE FRIENDLY FISHES: Making new friends at the Poor Knights Island marine reserve, Northland.

BEACH LIFE, ABEL TASMAN STYLE: Summertime at Totaranui, on the northern end of the Abel Tasman track.

Previous pages: SUMMIT DAY, McKINNON PASS: Trampers enjoy clear weather on the highest point of the Milford Track, Fiordland.

THE PICKET FENCE: Casting for the big one where the Waitahanui Stream meets Lake Taupo.

SOUNDS DOLPHIN: Dolphins accompany a sea kayaker in the Marlborough Sounds.

LAKE SPEEDSTER: An exhilerating jetboat ride on Lake Taupo.

MEET THE LOCALS: A juvenile fur seal welcomes sea kayakers off Tonga Island,
a marine reserve in Abel Tasman National Park.

PLAIN SAILING: A perfect day in the Bay of Islands, New Zealand's premier aquatic playground.

MOUNTAINS AND LAKES

CRATERS OF THE MOON: Steam billows forth at this thermal reserve just outside Taupo.
Previous pages: ALPINE SUMMER: Aoraki, Mt. Cook National Park with Lake Pukaki in the foreground.

SNOW CONE: Mt. Ngauruhoe in midwinter glory, with
Mt. Ruapehu, 2797m, towering behind.

DAIRY COUNTRY: Mt. Taranaki, 2518m, dominates the area around New Plymouth,
some of New Zealand's finest pastoral land.

HEIGHTS IN SUMMER: The Tongariro National Park in summer, showing the Tongariro Crossing track and the summits of Mt. Tongariro, Ngauruhoe and Ruapehu.

MYSTERIOUS LAKE ALEXANDRINA: Travellers on State Highway 1 often miss this pretty lake. It is located to the west of Mt John observatory, close to Lake Tekapo.

STORM BREWING: A summer storm builds at the head of Lake Rotoroa, Nelson Lakes National Park.

DAPPLED LIGHT NEAR DOG BOX CORNER: Sunlight plays across the hills near Burkes Pass, Mackenzie Country.

LILIES OF THE VALLEY: Summertime in the Hooker Valley, Aoraki, Mt. Cook National Park.

FROM THE WEST SIDE: Early light clears Mt Tasman, 3498m, viewed from Fox Glacier on the West Coast.

ADVENTURE COUNTRY: Heli hikers wait for a lift on the Fox Glacier.

RIVER OF ICE: The Franz Josef Glacier carves its way to the valley floor.

VIEW FROM THE TOP: Treble Cone ski area offers
magnificent views over Lake Wanaka

LADY OF THE LAKE: The TSS *Earnslaw* steams across Lake Wakatipu to Walter Peak Station.

WESTERN CONFLUENCE: The Landsborough meets the Haast River at Pleasant Flat.

Following pages: SOUTHERN REFUGE: Halfmoon Bay on Stewart Island.

GREAT SOUTHERN LAND: Lake Hakapoua meets Fouveaux Strait near Te Waewae Bay, on the wild southern coast.

Following pages: RED SKY AT NIGHT: In this case the red sky over Milford Sound brought solid rain for nearly two weeks.

ACKNOWLEDGEMENTS:

The majority of the images in this collection have been shot
on large format 6x12cm and 6x17cm panoramic cameras
using Fuji transparency film.

Exposure uses Fuji Film exclusively for its colour, sharpness and versatility. It definitely is the colour of our country.
Camera Specs: Linhof Technorama 6x17, Linhof Technorama 6x12, Fuji Panorama 6x17
Mamiya 645 Super, Hasselblad 35mm panorama, Nikonos underwater camera.

We would like to thank everyone who helped make this book happen.
Gray Clapham for his guidance and inspiration, the Team at Hanimex, Tony and Julie Monk of Heletranz, Robyn Langwell
and Bela Trussel-Cullen of *North and South*, Nicola Legat and Jenny Nicholls of *Metro*, and everyone else who
has told me where to go, in the nicest way possible.

And for my Mum and Dad. It's good to have you home.

Gareth Eyres, September 2003.